Living With Books

118 Designs for Homes and Offices

By Rita Reif

Quadrangle / The New York Times Book Company

Library of Congress Catalog Card Number: 72-96434

International Standard Book Number: 0-8129-0365-X

Newly revised and updated edition published 1973 by Quadrangle/The New York Times Book Company.

Contents

Introduction

Five years ago when this volume was completed there were empty spaces on some of the shelves of the four floor-to-ceiling book walls in my own home. Since then another wall of books has been added and my husband, two sons and I despair of finding a space for even the slimmest volume. I suspect that our plight is not unique. In fact, judging by communications I have had from those who have tried in vain to find this book, now long out of print, most people share our predicament.

To anyone born since the close of World War II, it might come as news that the abundance of books in homes and the dominant role they therefore play in decorating is a relatively recent development. Only a few decades ago books were too often confined to one or two glass-doored bookcases. The key in the lock testified to the rarity of the volumes and the pride of the owner. The key also testified to a far less liberal attitude than is held today on what could be read, how often and by which members of the family.

When the glass doors, lock and key disappeared, one of the most dramatic and pervasive changes in the appearance of the home began. Books began spreading up and across walls from the den and library to all rooms of the house.

These changes have quickened during, and partly as a result of, the boom in book sales which more than tripled in 15 years. More and more books, one of the most congenial problems ever visited upon the home, affects quarters large and small. The book boom has teased architects and designers and provoked many a homeowner to devise some highly imaginative solution to where and how the increasing number of books can be accommodated.

Two closely associated developments—collecting phonograph records and art—have found solutions in home libraries and their place in this book. Often the books, hi-fi components, recordings and art demand the same kind of installations and, in some rooms, the combination of all three elements adds character.

A passion for print is evidenced when the walls of a home or office groan with books, when the floors are stacked with books and even the plumbing is framed with books. But it also shows in a small child's room where a library of well-thumbed fairy tales, myths and adventure stories stands on shelves beside the bed.

Threaded through the pages of this book are some of the reasons why people collect books and how they live with them. There are the rooms that invite reading and those dedicated to work. There are kitchens where cookbooks consulted between chopping block and range result in feasts for the gods. There are foyers and hallways, dining rooms and bedrooms stuffed with books and there are other areas more modestly stocked.

Solutions to book storage problems exist in abundance. Where books can be stored—covering all or part of a wall, framing windows, doorways, and mantels or filling room dividers—depends on the individual's desires and needs.

What the professional and amateur installations shown here indicate is how wide-ranging and often elementary the answers actually are. Materials are equally diverse for today's home libraries. To explain how some of these designs and materials are engineered, there are several architectural drawings accompanying the photographs to assist professional and amateur carpenters.

The final chapter on ready-made furnishings represents a small sampling of the abundance of designs available today to those who do not opt for custom solutions.

As important as the design of the installations may be, it is the books themselves that really matter. The book owner's personality, as shown in his books, is what breathes life into the orange crates and paneling-framed installations in a room.

Hopefully, in this reprint of *Living With Books*, published in 1968 by The New York Times, the installations shown will assist others in working out their own solutions.

Rita Reif, January 1973

Around the House

A Warm Welcome

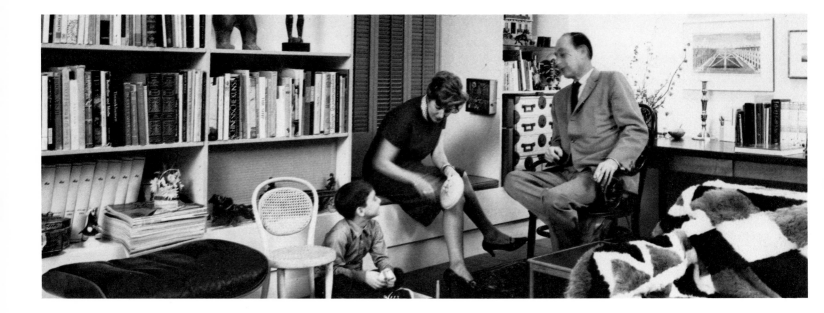

There is no want of books or imaginative ways to incorporate them in George Nelson's home high up over the streets of Manhattan. The industrial designer has spread the family library through every room of the converted servants quarters which the Nelsons call home. In a hall hard by the stairway near the entryway, he used space often overlooked by those with many volumes to accommodate. Here Mr. Nelson installed the Omni system which he designed during World War II and which became the first pole-supported vertical furniture. In it he and his wife keep novels, books on the decorative arts, other nonfiction and a few examples of folk art.

Far left: Custom installation in the living room covers an entire window wall and incorporates stationary and movable shelves and uprights. The contents reflect the eclectic tastes of Mr. and Mrs. Nelson, shown with their son Milo as they test the spin of a top. The window seat conceals air-conditioning ducts. Two loudspeakers for the hi-fi system are on the shelf behind Milo. Other components are housed elsewhere.

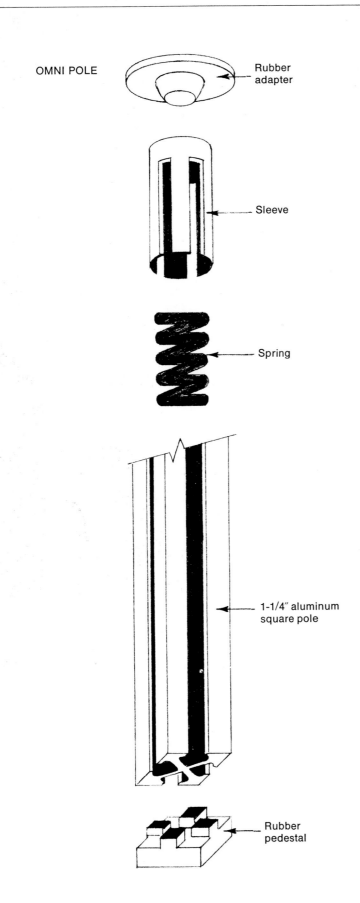

OMNI POLE

Rubber adapter

Sleeve

Spring

1-1/4″ aluminum square pole

Rubber pedestal

Preceding page: Aluminum poles extending from floor to ceiling are spaced 32 inches apart. 3/4-inch thick white plastic laminated shelves rest on aluminum brackets attached to the poles which are springloaded at the top to hold the entire arrangement in place. Other finishes are available for both the poles and shelves.

Under the Skylight

A carriage house that served ingloriously as a garage and bakery before J. Gordon Lippincott, industrial designer, found it and had it converted, has a two-story living room lit by day by a giant angled skylight of acrylic plastic. The 7-foot-high bookshelf unit directly below is of painted pine. Planked ceiling, exposed red brick walls, spare furnishings are in keeping with the character of the old building and the tastes of the Lippincotts. Recessed spotlights and an opal glass fixture light the room. Designed by Kenneth MacKenzie, architect.

Ship Lapping

Some people think nothing at all of tearing down walls and erecting new ones to accommodate a library. Hugh Newell Jacobsen, architect, is one of them. Here in the 1885 house he redesigned for his family in Georgetown, D.C., the space for the living room alcove library was stolen from the kitchen. But far more than shelf space was gained. The living room was given added depth and a new, arresting focal point. The bookcase, constructed of 3/8-inch white pine, was assembled like ship lapping and fixed in place with brads and glue. Shelves are 12 inches deep, 14 feet wide and of different heights for the variety of book sizes. The triptych painting by V. V. Rankine is lit by 44 three-watt flashlight bulbs.

On a Dais

The Victorian mansion Anthony Plunket Greene describes as a "hideous outside" has an inviting 20th century apartment inside that he and his wife, Mary Quant, the fashion designer, call home. What was the drawing room of the London house is the couple's living room. The 50-foot-long hall is dominated at one end by a raised dais where an 18th century French stove is flanked by painted plywood bookcases. (The stove is kept in working order to drive the chill from the 14-foot-high room when fog settles over the city.) The brass reading stand displays an ever-changing collection of drawings and art. Scarlet leather-covered sofas were designed for the room by Anthony Gregory, architect, who planned the apartment.

Doubled in Brass

Brass bookcases, copied from a Directoire étagère some years ago for the late Cole Porter, cover the living room wall and frame a doorway in the apartment of actor John Cronin. The brass frames are linked by crossed swords under the ebony shelves. The bookshelves were a bequest to Mr. Cronin from the composer who had had William Baldwin adapt the design and Frederick Victoria execute it for the Porters' apartment at the Waldorf-Astoria. Mr. Cronin chose to intensify the glitter of the brass system by painting the walls a shimmering black and adding sparkling accents in a steel and glass table and an abundance of crystal objects. J. Peter Heeren assisted the actor in decorating this room.

Hanging Shelves

An estimable collection of books on the decorative arts frames the dining area in Edward J. Wormley's New York apartment. The two walls of books conceal awkward beams. The wall at the rear had outsized structural columns on either side of a deep niche. Mr. Wormley, an interior designer and the dean of American furniture designers, filled the niche by suspending steel straps holding mahogany shelves from a new metal beam overhead. Each shelf supports 500 pounds of books. The rear of the niche contains a lighted panel that illuminates antiquities and modern art objects displayed on the cork shelf below the books. The wall at left has mahogany shelves cantilevered into the masonry, thus eliminating any visible supports. Mr. Wormley's library contains books on ancient Egypt, the Directories of Chippendale and Sheraton and works on the Art Nouveau movement and modern crafts.

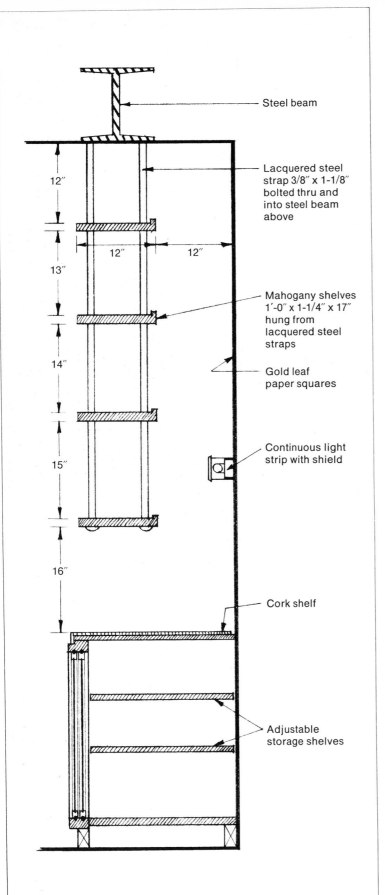

Steel beam

Lacquered steel
strap 3/8″ x 1-1/8″
bolted thru and
into steel beam
above

12″

12″   12″

13″

Mahogany shelves
1′-0″ x 1-1/4″ x 17″
hung from
lacquered steel
straps

14″

Gold leaf
paper squares

15″

Continuous light
strip with shield

16″

Cork shelf

Adjustable
storage shelves

Preceding page: Shelves are suspended from a steel beam in the ceiling by metal straps. Shelves are 17 feet long, 1 foot deep, 1-1/4 inches thick. Continuous light strip is attached to the wall behind the shelf above the display of art objects. The rear wall is covered with gold leaf paper. Adjustable shelves behind the sliding cane panels at the base of the unit are used for storage.

Majestic Egg Crates

Lacquered white cubicles shaped like egg crates line two walls in the dining room of Mr. and Mrs. Edward J. Mathews. They contain not eggs but books. Mrs. Mathews and her husband, an architect, have a broad range of reading interests. In this view of the room toward the windows, the area next to the kitchen door houses classical works that Mrs. Mathews inherited from her father, Henry Burchell, a classical scholar. Next come novels, nonfiction and 19th century works. Other volumes are accommodated on the wall facing the one shown. When the Mathews entertain at large dinner parties, they find that the books serve as sound absorbers as well as a decorative backdrop. The white-walled room with its green marble floor was designed by Mr. Mathews.

Sleeping and Reading

Few apartment dwellers can afford the luxury of a guest bedroom unless it can serve such other uses as a library and dining room. In Mr. and Mrs. Paul J. Smith's home the utter simplicity of a painted pine bookcase serves as a perfect background for all three functions—reading, dining and sleeping. The choice crafts collection of Mr. Smith, who is director of the Museum of Contemporary Crafts, and Mrs. Smith, who is the crafts editor of a women's magazine, is placed against colorful felt-covered panels which can be removed for a change of color, addition of books or to satisfy a whim. The white metal chandelier in the foreground casts a warm flickering light on the dining table below. The couple designed the shelves and helped finish them.

Books are always accessible in Albert Herbert's bed-sitting room. The bed disappears into the walnut wall but reading matter, which for this interior designer means books on the fine and decorative arts and magazines, is at all times within reach. The unit also contains storage space for the hi-fi system, television set and bedding on the left side of the bed section.

Wood-framed sliding doors conceal the entire contents of Alfred Wallenstein's library when it is not in use. In this bedroom the conductor and cellist keeps 3,000 scores, his 1710 Stradivarius cello, his tapes and phonograph records. Hi-fi components and a television set are installed on pull-out shelves at the far end of the wall. To reach the upper shelves of his library, Mr. Wallenstein had an oak table made into a ladder.

Twin bookcases flank the four-poster bed in Arlene Francis' New York apartment. The actress, wife of Martin Gabel, the producer-actor, likes to read scripts here and keeps the couple's large theater collection in the custom-designed shelving units. The ornamentation of the bookcases matches the turned post detail of the bed. Gold brocade is used for the coverlet, headboard and window shade of the room, which was designed by Blaine and Booth.

Pine shelves painted Bristol blue cover a wall surrounding doorways in the bed-sitting room of Stephen Spector, an art consultant. Mr. Spector, who designed the installation, uses the shelves for art books, catalogues and a collection of Worcester, Sèvres, Lowestoft and delft plates, jugs, bowls and vases.

In a sun-washed alcove in his bedroom, Alfred A. Knopf, the publisher, has spent countless hours over the last 40 years perusing reference works, typography books, volumes on history and the contents of his collection on the American West. The two book walls of the alcove are fitted with shelves and framed in wood. Since Mr. Knopf is a tall man, he can easily reach the top shelves in the alcove and those close to the ceiling in the sleeping area. In fact, the latter provide a decorative solution to the problem of storage. Furnishings in the English 17th century and Spanish Renaissance styles and the oriental rugs suit Mr. Knopf's Spanish-type stucco home in Westchester County.

More Bedrooms

Cane-paneled screens framed in rosewood slide across the window wall in the bedroom of Mr. and Mrs. Samson Berman, interior designers. Shelves on every other panel are of solid rosewood and are designed to support sculpture and books, regardless of weight. The screens move on nylon tracks and the cane-panels are backed by gold-colored silk. Designed by the owner and installed by Samson Berman Associates, Inc.

23

Where the Children Are

Books are just beginning to reveal their wonders to 8-year-old Leslie and 5-year-old Pamela. Both girls listen attentively when read to. Their father, Harold B. Ehrlich, installed the blue and white plastic-covered shelves, the worktable (which is fashioned from doors) and the ready-made cupboards, attaching them to the gypsum wall with metal standards and brackets. Metal plugs dipped in glue were used, Mr. Ehrlich explains, because plugs work out in gypsum walls unless firmly secured.

A wall that divides sometimes conquers storage problems in a home. In the room shown below, a painted plywood and pine divider separates the two boys who sleep on either side. It also provides storage for their books, toys, clothes and other possessions. Leslie, 12, keeps a large section set aside for mystery and adventure stories. Another shelf is reserved for a small but growing library of classics and other shelves for works on his special interests—anthropology, music and chess. Model trains are stored behind doors and, when set up, can run from the window to the door and on into his brother's room.

On the other side of the wall Timothy, 9, has similar accommodations for clothes and books and adequate space to push an impressive collection of cars about. His shelves, like his brother's, are adjustable. Small brass plugs hold them in place. For both boys the open door between their rooms is a welcome feature most of the time. But when tempers run high they appreciate not only being able to close the door, but the natural soundproofing provided by the double-thick wall of books. The wall was executed by Rudy Dezember.

25

Teen-agers seem to collect all sorts of objects and in Jeffrey Jablow's room they end up on the walnut bookshelves which are supported by metal strips and brackets. Scales, models, pennants, loving cups and a Joan Miró lithograph coexist with textbooks, mysteries, classics and current novels. The room was planned by Jeffrey in consultation with his mother, Evelyn Jablow, designer.

Double-decker beds and bookshelves were built into a bedroom in Mr. and Mrs. Carl Auböck's home in Vienna. Friends of the Auböck's two teen-age children sleep in this room during visits and seem to enjoy the reading matter—American and English paperbacks—as much as Mr. Auböck does. An architect, who studied in the United States, he designed the bleached ash shelves, which are held in place by steel pins and angle irons hidden on the far side of the wall.

Orange crates piled one on top of the other every which way, as children are wont to do, add up to an amusing, genuinely economical bookcase wall. Joan Kron, a designer, bolted these grocery boxes together and painted them white for the corner of a bedroom in her Philadelphia home. In addition to books, the crates hold folk art, outlandish decorations, blown-up photographs and the necessities of a vanity. 27

Painted white pine shelves are 12 inches deep. Car garage is 4 inches deep, 4 inches high backed by mirror. Lighting tubes are fluorescent. Norwegian maple laminated desk top is 16 feet long, 20 inches deep. Drawers are commercial metal file cabinets.

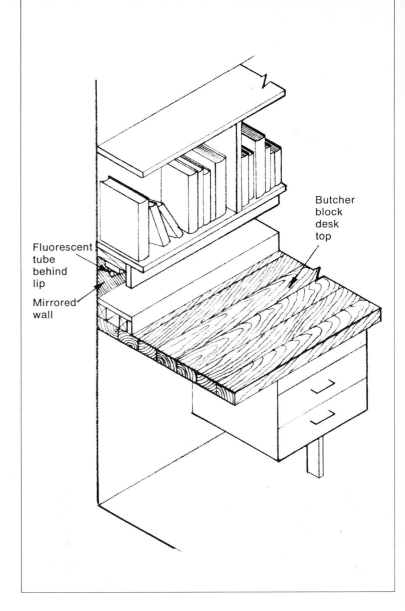

Butcher
block
desk
top

Fluorescent
tube
behind
lip

Mirrored
wall

Workshelf with Books

A wall-hung box for books, a niche for model cars and a place to study were designed by Hugh Newell Jacobsen, architect, for his two young sons. The white pine box is attached to a brick wall. Fluorescent tubes of light, concealed under the lip across the base of the box, illuminate the boys' mirrored miniature garage. The mirrored backdrop works the expected wonders in magnifying the play area. A butcher block desk, 16 feet long, sits on filing cabinets which are used to store school work and secret treasures.

In the Kitchen

Cooking in what was formerly the front parlor of their Brooklyn 19th century house, Laurie Maurer can share in the dinner conversation with her guests. Mrs. Maurer and her husband Stanley, both architects, designed this island of oak plywood and flooring to jut into what is now their dining room. Mrs. Maurer keeps her cookbooks in what she considers the most convenient place—the lowest shelf. On occasion her toddler daughter brings down a few books of her own to fill out the collection with variations on Mother Goose.

Glass shelves above the butcher block work counter store cook books and everyday china, cannisters and coffee pots. The well-ventilated galley-shaped room, has cupboards painted a soft green, white built-in wall oven and white painted trim. Shelves are supported by metal brackets and hung on metal strips attached to the back wall. Designed by George Nelson.

The galley-sized kitchen in the home of Mr. and Mrs. Melvin Stein is kept shipshape by the meticulous mistress of this household. Sugar pine shelves attached to the fir paneling above the sink accommodate spices and cookbooks. Cabinet doors below sink are red, a color repeated in cannisters, cooking utensils and other accessories. Designed by Stanley and Laurie Maurer, architects.

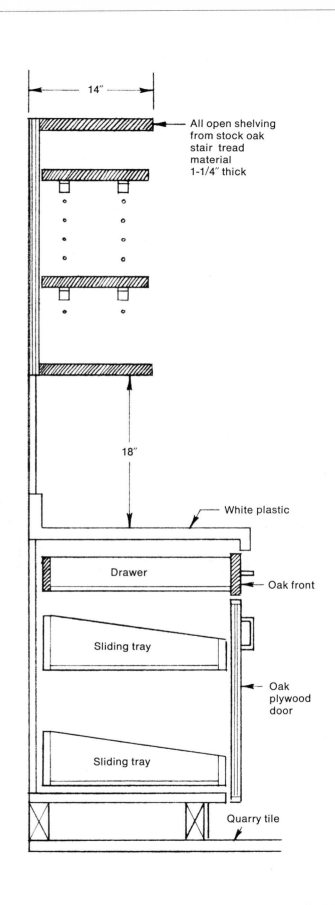

All open shelving from stock oak stair tread material 1-1/4″ thick

14″

18″

White plastic

Drawer

Oak front

Sliding tray

Oak plywood door

Sliding tray

Quarry tile

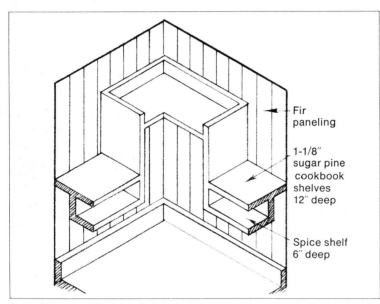

Fir paneling

1-1/8″ sugar pine cookbook shelves 12″ deep

Spice shelf 6″ deep

Preceding page: Shelves of 1-1/8-inch sugar pine are attached to fir paneling at top of 2-foot unit and behind spice shelf with metal cleat. Cookbook shelf is 12 inches deep, spice shelf is 6 inches.

Oak stair treads 1¼ inches thick, 14 inches wide used for open shelves which are adjustable. Shelves are placed 18 inches above white laminated plastic work counter. Drawer fronts are oak plywood.

Simple, Dominant, Useful

Open shelves of oak stair treads were the choice of Mrs. Winthrop Faulkner, whose husband, an architect, planned this kitchen for their Washington, D.C., home. "I was always hitting my head on cabinet doors," explains Mrs. Faulkner. The room is the family gathering place, and it is here that Dede, aged 10½ and the eldest of the couple's five children, experiments with cooking. One of Mrs. Faulkner's favorite volumes on the shelves here is Mrs. Beeton's Book of Household Management, published in 1912. Not only does she use it for creating a ravishing plum pudding, but she enjoys the outdated etiquette prescriptions. "Imagine getting advice on what your chauffeur should wear to hunting as opposed to the proper clothes for a funeral." Other amenities in this kitchen are the sheet cork backsplash to which Mrs. Faulkner affixes notes and the restaurant range which is large enough to cook a banquet.

More Kitchens

Blanche Thebom feels that the 80-year-old kitchen in her apartment across from New York's Carnegie Hall is something to sing about. The opera star modernized it by installing new equipment and having the ceiling lowered (the storage area above is reached by a ladder). Miss Thebom also had Betty Sanford Robie, her consultant, create a corner for menu planning with teak shelves for cookbooks. The shelves flanking the windows rest on metal brackets attached to metal strips on the wall.

Right: Cookbooks squirrel up in a kitchen wall niche created when the Robert B. Cadwalladers had their pre-Revolutionary barn remodeled a few years ago. The Stamford, Conn., home of the executive at Knoll Associates, furniture producer, and his family has a spacious cooking area with wall ovens adjoining the book niche. Robin's egg blue bentwood chairs are used for dining under a wall hung with a variety of curiosities.

Below: A hallway connecting kitchen and living room in the Brooklyn home of Ronald Clyne proved a natural place for the commercial artist's library. Mr. Clyne, who designed the interiors of the house, is a meticulous man who keeps his cookbooks at the kitchen end of the middle shelves, within easy reach when preparing dinner. The oak shelves were set into the wall during construction. Laminated plastic surfaces are used throughout the kitchen.

The kitchen in the New Jersey home of Mr. and Mrs. Wer-
ner J. Fleischmann was modeled on a Swiss stübli, a small, cozy
room often found in an Alpine inn. Although the century-old
beams and siding from a barn that Mr. Fleischmann had razed
give the room the stübli-like warmth and intimacy, the area is
far from small. One idea borrowed not from Switzerland but
England by the Swiss-American toy importer is the iron grat-
ing behind the bookshelf, above his home bar The gate was
patterned after those lowered over the bar in some British pubs
at closing time. At the Fleischmanns' the iron bars are immobile
but serve to hold the cookbooks in place.

Decorative Solutions

Around the Fireplace

It is more than happy coincidence that the recesses on one or both sides of the living room chimney breast have come to be a favorite place for bookshelves. After all there are few pleasures to compare with settling down, good book in hand, to read beside a healthy fire. In the Vienna home of Carl Auböck, an architect, the ancient idea is updated in an ultra-modern manner. Three shelves extend from the chimney to the window wall at right. Invisible supports placed 12 inches apart keep the shelves from sagging under the weight of the books. And, on the platform below is an ample supply of logs to feed the fire whenever a member of this family decides to curl up in a black leather chair to lose himself in history, fiction or fantasy.

Hardy Amies' books on herbology are among his most prized and frequently thumbed possessions. The fashion designer had pine shelving units created to flank the fireplace—and, as can be seen through the mirror, to frame the Henry Moore printed textile on the opposite wall. The slab-like oiled pine sides of the bookshelves stand free of the room's side walls to give the units a feeling of lightness and strength. The lower shelves are adjustable, upper ones are fixed to support the side members. A bar is installed on the left side under a marble counter. The hi-fi is on the right. It is here that Joan Sutherland, the opera diva, who is a friend and neighbor of Mr. Amies, comes to listen to opera recordings. Mr. Amies' library documents interests other than the culinary, aromatic and medicinal virtues of herbs (an interest registered in his green garden below the French windows of this 1880 house in Kensington, London). He has a large collection of travel books and enjoys perusing an enviable section devoted to art and antiques. The room and many of its furnishings were designed by Michael Raymond of Colefax & Fowler Associates.

Most of the wall space in the New York apartment of Leo Castelli, art gallery owner, is reserved for paintings and other works of art. Consequently, only a small portion of Mr. Castelli's books can be accommodated in the living room. In the space to the left of the fireplace, art books and French novels share the painted plywood shelves with components and phonograph records. On the Early American refectory table are an old brass ship's clock and a ceramic head by Roy Lichtenstein, the pop artist. Over the mantel is a Jasper Johns flag painting.

41

Islands

In this Portland, Ore., home, Richard A. Campbell, an architect, constructed a teak-framed, teak-veneered plywood shelf above the steel fireplace. The books are not affected by the heat because the hearth is well insulated. Hi-fi speakers serve as dividers separating standard reference works from the writings of such authors as Arnold Toynbee and Will Durant. Mr. Campbell, his wife and children like the convenience of having the books over the fireplace, on the far side of which is the kitchen.

When the walls of a home are already covered with bookshelves, new devices must be found to house new volumes. In the case of Francis Robinson, a divider backing the sofa was selected as the solution. The assistant manager of the Metropolitan Opera has allocated every available inch of wall, closet and kitchen cabinet space to house his 7,000 books on the theater and the opera. Aside from containing his albums and reference materials, the divider-bookcase serves to create two distinct areas in Mr. Robinson's living room. Mementos of stars, such as the Caruso walking stick that Mr. Robinson holds and the autographed pictures of Cornelia Otis Skinner and Leontyne Price on the divider, appear throughout the apartment.

Peninsula

Rooms, like people, often lead double lives. By day they must often serve for work. By night they function for relaxation. In cases where living quarters and business are combined, as in Marjorie Neikrug's art gallery, the two functions need separation. A divider unit with the near side facing her office, the far side the gallery-living room was the neat solution of Charles Gwathmey and Richard Henderson, designers. The birch plywood unit is stacked with books and art materials in the work area and fitted with drawers and shelves for linens, silver, hi-fi and television on the opposite side.

Birch plywood unit is 56 inches high, 120 inches long, 25 inches deep. Book sections are 10 inches deep, 24 and 48 inches wide. Opposite side has 48-inch-wide bar section, 48-inch-wide TV-hi-fi section and a panel of drawers 24 inches wide.

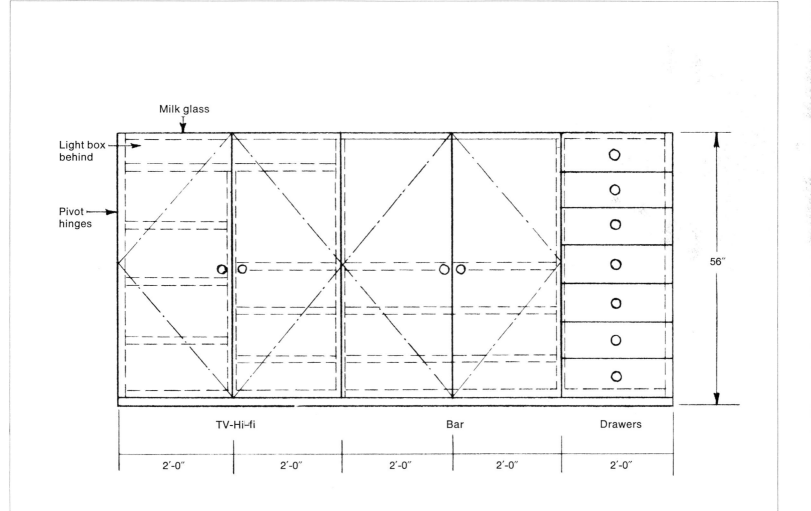

Milk glass

Light box behind

Pivot hinges

56″

TV-Hi–fi   Bar   Drawers

2'-0″   2'-0″   2'-0″   2'-0″   2'-0″

Boxes Pure and Simple

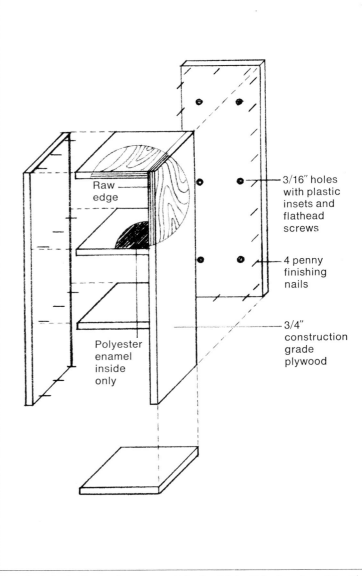

Raw edge

3/16" holes with plastic insets and flathead screws

4 penny finishing nails

3/4" construction grade plywood

Polyester enamel inside only

Box of 3/4-inch plywood measures 48 inches high, 12 inches deep, 18 wide. 3/16-inch holes drilled in back panel. Inside of shelves painted with polyester enamel, outside left natural with raw, laminated edges exposed.

Boxes, big and small, are one of the simplest ways to house books, records and art objects. Hugh Hardy, an architect, used five pieces of ¾-inch plywood for each of the boxes, leaving the layered edges exposed to add pattern interest to the arrangement. Even the cord of the hanging lamp and the stripe on the wall under the shelves is part of the tongue-in-cheek assemblage. These open-front crates are child's play to make, the architect claims. And as for installation he suggests that two holes be drilled in the wall into which plastic cups are inserted. When the boxes are fastened by screws into the plastic cups, the cups automatically grip the screws firmly.

Let Them Hang

    In the entryway of Dr. William S. Greenspon's New York apartment-office, an angled shelf was hung on the wall to hold magazines and small books. The foyer doubles as a waiting room for the patients of the psychiatrist yet it avoids the look of an office. Dr. Greenspon constructed the simple shelf, using plywood painted black and attaching it to the wall with angle irons. The shelf measures 41 inches long, 14⅛ wide. It has a 2⅞-inch lip to keep reading matters from sliding off.

The unit hanging above the bed in Mr. and Mrs. Stanley Poler's one-room apartment is one of two bookcases that were cut from a single sheet of plywood measuring 96 by 48 inches. It is 64 inches high, 32 inches wide, 8 inches deep and is decorated with inlay that the couple took from an 1813 church which was being demolished in Brooklyn. Mr. Poler, an engineer, built the unit as well as all the furniture in the room. The couple are inveterate scavengers of 19th-century architectural elements, many of which decorate their home. When not working or studying (Mrs. Poler is a law student) they sometimes peruse their albums of snapshots documenting century-old New York buildings.

The boxy walnut units that Gordon Parks designed and had a carpenter make for the bedroom-studio of his Beekman Place apartment in New York are hung on concealed wood strips attached to the wall. The photographer, author and composer keeps novels, music, prose and poetry here and works at this desk which was formerly in the Spanish Embassy in London.

Store-Bought and Floor to Ceiling

Three ready-made bookcases purchased in a department store stretch floor to ceiling in Tennessee Williams' skyscraper apartment. They stand side by side and appear to be one large unit because of the strips of molding that are nailed to them before they were painted brown. They fit like a glove between two examples of the ubiquitous columns that plague occupants of post-World War II buildings. Mr. Williams surrounds himself with palm trees, a bust of Byron, a glass menagerie on a table top, a ruby-glass oil lamp, brown velvet sofas and the books that he is forever giving away to callers who evidence even the slightest interest in their contents.

Right: Everyone ducks when Sam P. Karas, his wife or any of his three daughters takes a pole to dislodge a book from the upper shelves of this library. But a ladder is necessary to return books to their places. The 26-foot high room in this Monterey, Calif., home doubles as a bedroom for two of the Karas' daughters when they are home from college. It is also where the family entertains (Mr. Karas, a wholesale butcher, is a master barbecuer) with musical accompaniment from the balcony. When a local guitarist is not available to perform on the landing, all members of this stage-struck family take turns. The compact house, which cost $22,000, was designed by Charles W. Moore, chairman of the School of Architecture at Yale University, and his partner William Turnbull Jr.

Door and Window Frames

Books create a rich mosaic of color and pattern in the entryway of Mr. and Mrs. Harry N. Abrams' New York home. Two walls serve as a repository for works of fiction and the humanities, a small part of the art book publisher's collection of 5,000 volumes. The dark gray painted plywood shelves perform functionally as well as decoratively by visually unifying the wall spaces broken by doorways.

Right: The only colors in this white-on-white soaring, two-story-high living room are in the stained glass panels and stunning book installation which frames the leaded glass windows, warming this imposing space. Even Sugar and Andrew, the sister and brother Persian cats who live here, are as white as the wool rugs, the shimmering vinyl upholstery and the ceramic tile floor. David W. Beer, the architect who designed this room and its seating units, had the second hand piano painted white; the same high gloss, wipe-clean finish as was used on the square-armed sofas. Hi-fi components, phonograph records and books, books and more books are all accommodated in the library walls. Naturally, the volumes perused most frequently occupy the lowest shelves. Indeed, so far, the top three shelves, which are virtually unreachable, still contain the volumes purchased just to fill them.

Gene Moore saves money by making and painting the pine shelves in his apartment himself—and then he uses the money he saves to buy even more books. For over a decade Mr. Moore, who designs Tiffany's windows, has been adding to the shelves on which he keeps his collection of books and records and a record player, tuner and amplifier. Speakers are hidden behind the cloth panels in low cupboards elsewhere in this room.

Wall to Wall

Although 3,000 of Leo Lerman's books were sold recently, his pine shelves and fabric-swathed tables still cannot contain the remainder. The overflow, as under a table here, is alphabetically arranged according to the classification of the room. "Proust upstairs, Renaissance down," says Mr. Lerman, author and Victorianophile, who has lined the walls and surrounded the plumbing of his four-story house with volumes on art, history, literature and the foibles of mankind. From his horsehair loveseat he can close his eyes and visualize exactly where every book is placed. In this parlor with its Staffordshire figures in niches, the subject is English life and letters and the only intruders are a bevy of cookbooks on a shelf within easy reach of a man who likes to cook well and dine sumptuously.

Dadoes are a logical place to deposit books in rooms devoted to art, leaving the upper wall for paintings and sculpture. In the apartment of Harry N. Abrams, the art book publisher, books occupy the lower part of the wall on plywood shelving units painted white. The top of the bookcase in the Abrams' "Pop Art" room is used to display several works by modern artists. And on the wall above is the "Oh Jeff" painting by Roy Lichtenstein.

Dado

Unlikely Corners

An eyrie in the master bedroom of this modern home, an anomaly in a contemporary house, overlooks some of Connecticut's most picturesque open fields. From her perch on the window seat, the mistress of this house observes the vagaries of the seasons before settling down most every afternoon to read, knit or rest. The triangular dormer window and bookshelves under the eaves were part of Ann Renehan's architectural plan which her clients enthusiastically endorsed. The far wall is white, the niche terra cotta and the bedwall is covered with natural-colored burlap.

Left: The trapezoidal molding shaping the bookcase in front of a window in the London apartment of Jean-Claude Ciancimino, an antiques dealer, follows the line of the mansard roof. Mr. Ciancimino collects rare books and settles them with an equally impressive collection of old musical instruments, marble obelisks, a 16th century chess board and a Venetian mask.

57

Strips of glittering steel tacked to the wood facade of the bookcase wall in this Manhattan living room blend with other sparkling elements. A shimmering lacquered floor and angular table—both white, an old mirror, a mercury glass-based lamp and a vinyl-covered screen complete the scheme. The charcoal painted shelves hold art and design books and hi-fi components. The speaker for the system is over the doorway, the amplifier and tuner on a shelf at left. The room was designed by Harry M. Schule and John McCarville of Schule-McCarville Designs.

Around Doors, Over Windows

By sacrificing part of a window wall, the Robert B. Cadwalladers gained a bookshelf in the living room of their Stamford, Conn., 1760 home. The converted barn interior shown here banished livestock and hay 40 years ago when the humanizing elements of a stone fireplace, windows and an adjoining kitchen and dining room were added. Mr. Cadwallader, vice president of Knoll Associates, furniture producers, added finishing details. Red cedar boxes in pipes in corner and above bookcases. Spruce scaffold board was stained to match beams for the bookshelves and frame.

Classical moldings do as much for some book installations as seasoning does for soup. Here in the eminently comfortable library of Mollie Parnis, the fashion designer, the moldings dress up plain painted bookcases flanking the doorway contributing a necessary cachet to the inviting setting. Miss Parnis, who is the widow of Leon Livingston, furnished the room with squashy seating, fine art and an abundance of books on art and 20th century literature. Mrs. Livingston collects limited editions of 20th century authors which she keeps here and in two rooms on the floor above. The painted plywood bookshelves square off at the top of the doorway and hold hi-fi speakers faced with cream moire grille cloths. These amenities and the decor of the setting were the work of William Baldwin, the decorator.

Under the Window

A passion for books has led, indeed forced, Mr. and Mrs. Alexander Liberman to incorporate them in every room of their New York home. The artist and magazine editor credits his wife, Tatiana, with the design of all the shelving units, which are purposely simple. The dimensions of the boxy bookcases vary from room to room, but the material—plywood painted the color of the walls—remains the same throughout. Here in the living room the arrangement is sill-high, extending the length of the windows. A screen by Vertès, the artist, conceals the phonograph records and hi-fi equipment, which stand on shelves at the end of the unit. French novels, all paperbacks, and the small art works contribute contrast and a variety of interesting patterns.

Into the Wall

Not everyone has walls thick enough to permit carving out a book niche. But Stephen H. Kiviat, architect, does. With the blessing of his landlord he cut a hole in the living room wall for his modest library. The interior was then lined with white plaster. Oak shelves stained and varnished to match the wood trim were installed. A second niche was carved out to the left of the first. The masculine belted armchairs here by Mario Bellini are of dark blue suèded cotton. The silk screen is by Stephen Gottlieb.

Libraries and Dens

Heavy Elegant
Light Elegant

Away in an alcove of his Milan living room, Giuseppe Fiocchi quietly thumbs through books and magazines on economics, travel and photography. The library corner here houses only a small percentage of the Italian businessman's books, but it is to this cozy hideaway that he comes to read. The shelves, all movable, are lacquered an egg shell color. Maximum use was made of side walls and, to increase a sense of intimacy while gaining more storage space, an archway was added. Carla Venosta, who planned this room, also designed the dark brown, plastic-framed settee covered in natural leather. Books and a red, blue and white carpet by David Hicks, the London decorator, spice the setting with color.

High above the streets of Brussels, at the top of the glass-walled bank building he owns, is the penthouse-library of Baron Leon Lambert. The volumes include textbooks from the Baron's days at Yale, art books in three languages and works by Racine, Voltaire, Stendhal and Molière. A collection of Pre-Columbian, Congolese, Japanese and other Oriental art objects graces the teak-veneered adjustable shelves. The library, which was designed by Skidmore, Owings & Merrill, opens onto a salon and dining room and is often used for entertaining. Tape-recorded music is played on equipment installed below the window. Late Regency chairs, Saarinen pedestal tables and an early-19th-century desk complete the furnishings.

In the Grand Manner

Left: Pauline Trigère, the fashion designer, covets and carefully selects leather-bound books designed by contemporary artists. The same care governed her design suggestions for the library corner of her New York apartment. The classic moldings, arched facing of windows (not shown), boiserie and period furnishings were her ideas. A closet with a glass door displays a collection of spice bottles. The jewel-colored bindings on the shelves are set off by a neutral background.

Right: Mrs. Otto Koerner's library-living room is paneled in smoked fir and furnished with Gothic and Renaissance works of art. The shelves, which are adjustable, are filled with reference books on art, music, literature and history and reflect Mrs. Koerner's wide-ranging interests. A founder of Vancouver's International Festival and a trustee of the National Gallery of Canada, she prepares catalogues in this room for art shows in the Vancouver Gallery. Speakers for the hi-fi system are concealed behind two fabric panels.

Grander Still (Preceding Spread)

The great hall shown on the preceding two pages was once the domain of the late A. S. W. Rosenbach, the book dealer. Now it is part of the duplex home of his successor, John F. Fleming. Mr. Fleming kept the manorial air of the room, left the Spanish weavings and Italian copes, Renaissance mantel, outsized library table and Chippendale and Queen Anne chairs. The glass doors of the bookcases protect their contents from the dust of New York City.

Each of the leather-covered rare volumes is periodically treated with a thoroughly mixed application of half neatsfoot oil and half lanolin. This, plus polishing, preserves the life and luster returns of bindings that date from the 15th century.

As choice as the books are such furnishings as the Austrian Savonnerie rug on which Napoleon's Josephine walked in her summer home at Malmaison. The lampshade on the table is made of parchment leaves from an old volume of Chaucer's Canterbury Tales. The lectern in a corner of the room, shown above, is a Renaissance piece.

A structure enclosing a garden on three sides and housing close to 60,000 volumes is a bookworm's dream. For Joseph and Muriel Buttinger (he is a scholar and author in the social sciences) it is a reality. Their New York home rests on a foundation of books—two stories and a basement filled with works related to his interests. The floors above are the couple's home. In the areas shown below and left, Felix Augenfeld, architect, chose blue metal bookcases, a wooden book truck and card file, all obtained from office supply companies. For softening effects he relied on color—the yellow doors on the cabinets and red upholstery on the chairs. Oak treads and a cheery railing enhance the blue steel circular staircase.

Duplex

Factory Shelves

The attic library in this New York home was planned by Elaine Lustig Cohen, a graphics designer. She arranged 15,000 volumes on art, design, philosophy and the history of ideas in an Art Metal shelving system which stands free of walls and windows. Each of the panels at the end of the shelves is painted a different brilliant color—gold, orange, pink, red. Lighting tubes are hung from the ceiling. Like the other equipment, the metal filing cabinets come from an office supply house, but they are covered with a handsome weaving.

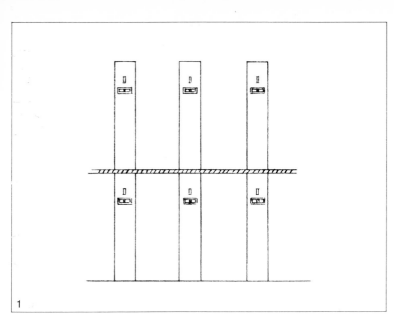

1

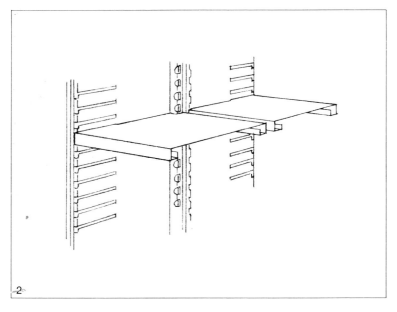

2

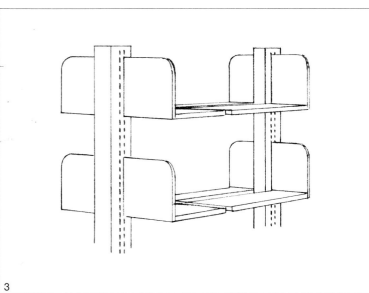

3

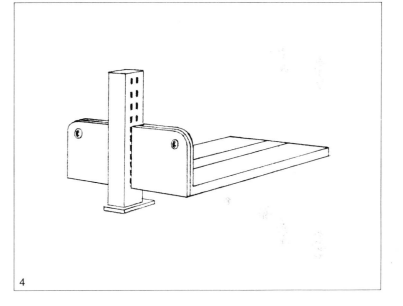

4

Among the steel components of Art Metal shelving are (1) full height end panels for single-tier and double-tier bookstacks; (2) U-shaped shelf supports slotted at 1-inch intervals to permit adjustability; (3) bracket-type stacks which vary in depth for various sizes of books and (4) bracket-type bases which leave an opening at the base.

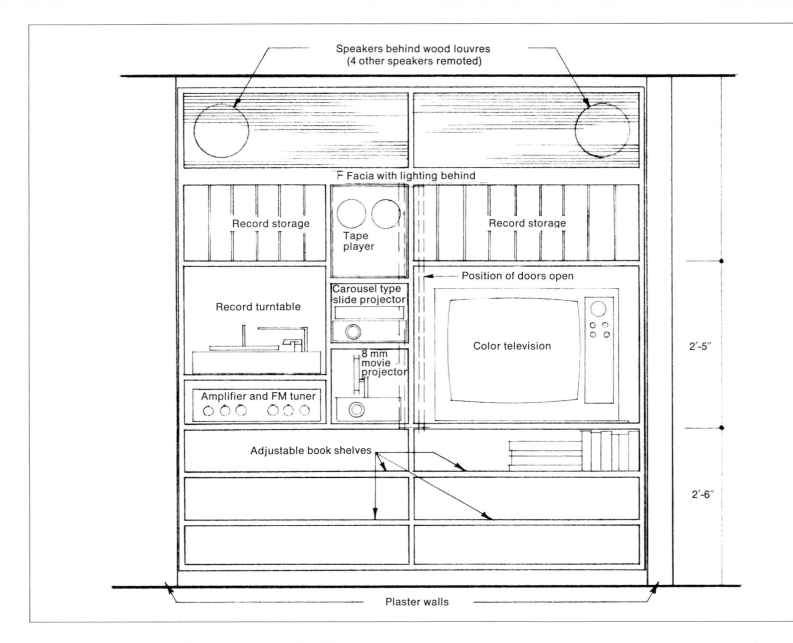

Speakers behind wood louvres
(4 other speakers remoted)

F Facia with lighting behind

Record storage

Tape
player

Record storage

Carousel type
slide projector

Position of doors open

Record turntable

8 mm
movie
projector

Color television

Amplifier and FM tuner

Adjustable book shelves

2'-5"

2'-6"

Plaster walls

Teak wall, 10 feet long, 24 inches deep, has adjustable shelves at base.
Center section is subdivided for television, hi-fi, record storage and
projectors. Top part has speakers hidden behind louvres in back of ship's
models.

The ship models on the upper shelf of the teak storage wall in Mr. and Mrs. Albert Kennerly's Manhattan home reveal something of their great interest in sailing. In the unit below the shelf, Mr. Kennerly, an architect with Fordyce Hamby & Kennerly Associates, designed storage space for audio-visual equipment. A television set, hi-fi components, phonograph records and slide and film projectors are concealed behind the doors, which have matched teak veneers. The adjustable bookshelves at the base of the unit contain both fiction and reference works, supplementing a collection in the Kennerlys' country home in Sag Harbor, L.I. The map above the sofa is Italian, circa 1600. The one under glass on the table is 18th century.

Nautical Library

Dens

This den is two stories high and dramatically illuminated by shafts of sunlight. In it the members of a New Canaan, Conn., family read and listen to music. The 20-foot-long bookshelves on the wall and the cabinets below for hi-fi equipment and record storage are of white birch plywood. Five sections for books and 10 cabinets were specified by Ulrich Franzen, architect. The birch has two coats of lacquer treated with steel wool to give it a matte finish. The cabinet top is impervious to water and alcohol. The birch is ¾-inch plywood save the record dividers, which are ¼-inch thick. The hi-fi speakers are covered with natural cane panels.

Magazines accumulate all too quickly as Mr. and Mrs. Donald Blinken well know. The painted plywood bookshelf wall in their den was planned with an eye to organizing periodicals as well as books. The Blinkens have diverse if sympathetic interests—Mr. Blinken, a stockbroker, is an art collector; Mrs. Blinken represents composers and a dance company. Both collect reading material related to their specialties. The room was designed by John W. Bedenkapp.

Books at Work

Would You Believe a Closet?

Nicos Zographos converted a coat closet off the living room of his apartment into a combination office and library. The designer arranged shelves to store books, magazines, records, phonograph, tape recorder, tuner and amplifier as well as design drawings. Dividers spaced fairly closely together keep the records upright. Mr. Zographos even leaves his telephone in the closet. Best of all, when his working day is over he merely closes the folding doors to his office and is home in his living room.

Or a Hall?

A hallway off the living room in a 19th-century New York brownstone serves as an office at home for John W. Bedenkapp, an architect. Composition wood shelves supported by metal brackets attached to four metal strips line the charcoal-colored walls to accommodate books on architecture, art and other subjects. The desk has a white plastic laminated work surface. The rosewood chair is Burmese of the Regency period. Two of the drawings are by Picasso and Giacometti.

Out-of-the-Way Places

Above: In this windowless cubicle, a converted second kitchen in his Greenwich Village apartment, a drawing board is always at hand for work, a chess board for relaxation, for George Lois. The executive art director and partner in an advertising agency says that here, in the still of the night, he gets some of his most creative ideas. If reference books are needed they are close by in the Danish shelving system. And when inspiration is absent there is always the chess board and a problem to solve.

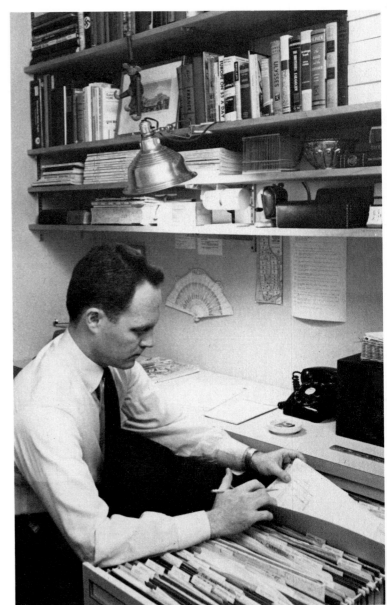

There are books where the coats once hung in what was the entryway to the apartment of Mr. and Mrs. Clyde R. Rich Jr. Mr. Rich, an architect, had the closets removed from the wall to create this well-engineered office. In the alteration an awkward architectural problem was solved: recesses on either side of a column in the center of what is now the book wall were covered with a false wall above the work table. Below the table, however, these recesses accommodate double-deep filing cabinets. The desk chair is a relic of a turn-of-the-century schoolroom.

Above: A room within a room fabricated of backless bookshelves and tatami matting was Lanier Graham's solution to creating a work area at home. The exterior of the cube adds architectural interest to the living room and houses the joint book collection of Mr. and Mrs. Graham. But when you turn the cube inside out Mr. Graham's work area comes to life. It is here that the design problems he carries home from his office at the Museum of Modern Art often find solution.

Behind an oak headboard, Dr. Richard Hinman, a chemist, has created an arched unit for his books. His interests are wide-ranging and their scope is reflected by the contents of the shelves (a preponderance of art books plus novels, biography, history, reference works) and the boat plans he holds. A 17th century vargueno, a multi-drawered unit, hangs on the wall over a Spanish Renaissance table. The room was designed in consultation with Lee Berman.

Studios

The home of Richard Lindner, the artist, contains a bedroom that doubles as a library and work area. Mr. Lindner does his sketching while seated on the three-legged stool. Canvases, painted in the adjoining studio, are stored along the library wall. The entire storage unit, designed by Felix Augenfeld, an architect friend, uses components manufactured by the Kason Hardware Corporation. Steel spring tension poles are combined with wood shelves. In this all white room, color is provided by the paintings, the books (fine arts, humanities and poetry) and an orangey-red and yellow African rug.

The studio in which Leonard Bernstein composes and prepares scores for New York Philharmonic performances is a hushed room whose draperies are usually drawn against the sun. Opera, orchestral and choral works, albums of press clippings, phonograph records and reference books fill the shelves on two walls. The dark tan of the walls and the deep brown leather chair add to the subdued atmosphere of the studio, which is on the ground floor of Mr. Bernstein's home. The red lacquered liquor cabinet incorporated into the Royal System shelving components at left was painted to order.

Shelves of 1-1/8 inch thick by 12 inches deep are fir stair treads. Shelves sit on 2 by 2-inch wood strips attached to back brick wall by screws in metal anchors in wall. Verticals of 2 by 12-inch fir are attached to shelves in three parts by wood dowels glued in place.

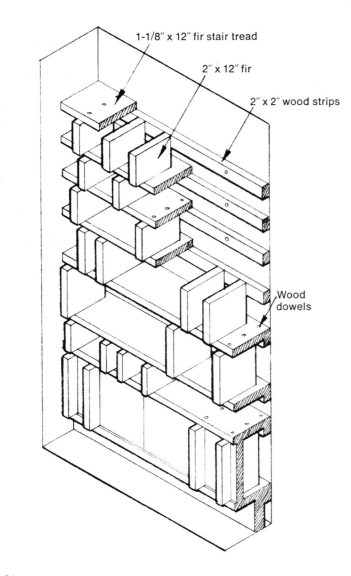

1-1/8″ x 12″ fir stair tread

2″ x 12″ fir

2″ x 2″ wood strips

Wood dowels

Fir stair treads were used for wall-to-wall installation of bookshelves in the home office of Stanley and Laurie Maurer, architects. Shelf heights were arranged according to book sizes, (largest in center, smallest at top for paperbacks.) The vertical dividers are fixed permanently in place, doweled to the shelves to keep books separated. They add to shelf support and reduce the possibility of sagging while contributing an attractive pattern to the wall. Cabinets at base are used for storing house plans and work materials.

A free standing, double-deep bookcase usable from both sides functions also as a room divider and for storage of work materials for Adolf Knüppel, German architect and sculptor. The jagged-edged structure is fabricated of chipboard panels painted white that simply plug together like a child's cardboard block set or the dividers in an egg crate. Mr. Knüppel designed the structure for his apartment in Münster, Westphalia, as he did all other furnishings including the dining room table seen at the far end of the room. The low-cost modular system which he hopes will be manufactured in the future has the advantage of being easily dismantled and erected in different positions.

Chipboard and Steel

What works in a warehouse works in the home office of Mrs. Yung Wang, architect, who has equipped her work area with second hand, warehouse-type metal bookcases. The units were painted white and are 12 inches deep, 7 feet high. Two more units on the far side of the wall hold more books. Mrs. Wang works on a desk-top made of a solid core oak door measuring 7 feet long, 30 inches wide. The base of the desk is a pair of pedestals used for restaurant tables.

A Useful Detail

A working library at the top of Adele Simpson's New York townhouse is stocked with a creditable selection of works on the decorative arts and, in particular, fashion. The dress designer had the plywood installation made with adjustable shelves. Pull-out workshelves run the length of the wall of books and labels serve as a guide to Mrs. Simpson, her husband and partner Wesley, and the students and other designers who are invited to use the library.

By day the home office of Frederick Gorree, architect, occupies a corner of his apartment-living room. A desk, bentwood chair and books furnish the area. Shelves are of ¼-inch-thick glass, supported by metal standards and brackets. By night the black laminated plastic-topped desk on stainless steel legs, is used for dining. Additional chairs are drawn up from the adjoining living room.

Still Standard

In a Factory

For Ivan C. Karp, author and art gallery director, life in a converted factory features all the comforts of home. Pine shelves were put up on the walls and pop art and other works were hung. Books are arranged systematically by shelf, with volumes about art on the bottom, then sociology and psychology, physics and astronomy and finally fiction. Mr. Karp's own book, Doobie Doo, would go on the top shelf. Wood dividers between books can be moved at will and serve to hold them in place. Records are stored in the closed cupboards.

At the end of the silk-paneled wall facing David Rockefeller's desk in the Chase Manhattan Bank, the white-lacquered shelves hold books and a choice selection of the banker's art collection—primitive carvings, fine porcelains and antiquities. The floor-to-ceiling installation has adjustable shelves resting on metal brackets. Mr. Rockefeller's desk, the upholstered sofa and chairs and the conference table were designed by Skidmore, Owings & Merrill, architects, who did the entire office and building.

Far From the Crowd

Not Homey

During the recent remodeling of the offices of Dean Witter & Co., stockbrokers, more efficient operation of its research division was planned. A wire lathe and plaster wall of bookshelves was made the focus of the Wall Street concern's serene, well-lighted library. All the bound research materials required by the staff are accommodated on the shelves. Two lighted niches between the three book sections allow researchers to consult reference books without having to take them back to their desks. Don Eliasen of Duffy, Inc., space planners, was responsible for designing the changes.

The walls between the offices of editors and division directors at Grosset & Dunlap, publishers, are bookshelves on one side and tack-boards on the other. The 7-foot-high dividers of white birch topped with glass provide privacy while permitting sunlight to filter through the whole area. At the entrance to the office of Lawrence Reeves, director of the school and library division, Manuel Siwek, the company's president pauses. The only thing Mr. Reeves doesn't like about his office, which is furnished with Marcel Breuer chairs and tan carpeting, is the absence of a door to bang.

Books, Hi-Fi and Art

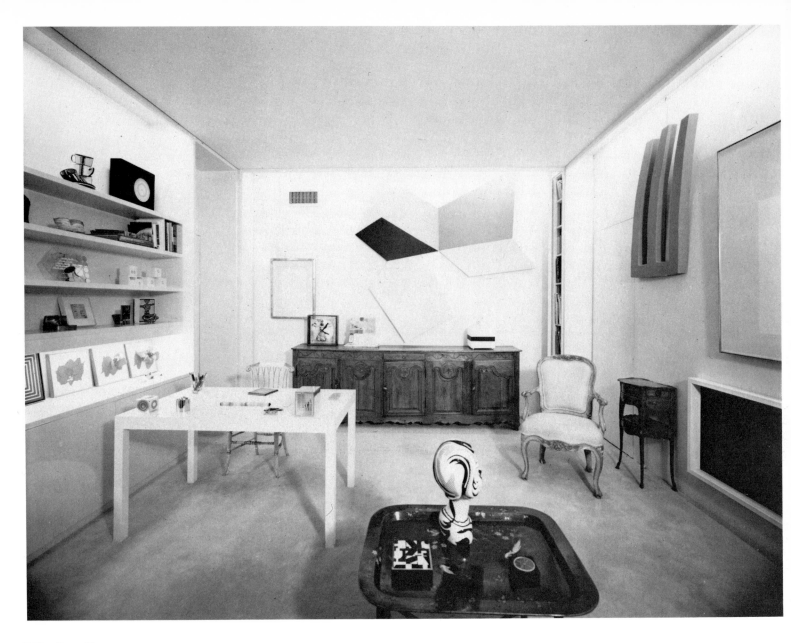

Tight Squeeze

Books, art and architecture all play an important part in the library of Mr. and Mrs. Burton G. Tremaine Jr. The Connecticut industrialist and his wife keep volumes that are indispensable to their art interests on the shelves on the wall and in a fake column, at right, where eight additional shelves are adjustable. This column matches a structural column, at left, and was constructed to give the room symmetry when the ceiling was lowered and lighting installed. The kinetic, pop and op art on the shelves includes the stacked cup sculpture by Roy Lichtenstein. Over the French Provincial cabinet is a construction by Charles Hinman. Above the fireplace at right is a Josef Albers painting. The room was designed by John W. Bedenkapp.

Right: Narrow niches on either side of Otto Preminger's fireplace are filled with rosewood units for books and hi-fi components. The components for the stereophonic system including a phonograph in a pull-out drawer, disappear from sight when not in use behind the door at right. The motion picture director-producer has a few paintings from his estimable art collection here, namely a Pierre Soulages over the mantel and a Paul Klee on the wall, at right.

A hall closet in this passageway between the foyer and bedroom in Stephen Spector's apartment was replaced with a storage wall for books and art objects. Pine shelves cover the upper wall, placed 18 inches apart to accommodate the outsized books, the terra cotta sculptures and two Directoire clocks. The 9-foot high corridor was lowered to 8 feet with a fiberglass ceiling, above which incandescent lighting strips were installed. Lower section has a glass top with lighting below to accent the baroque sculptures of saints. Louvered wood doors conceal cupboards where the art consultant stores gallery and auction catalogues and reference books.

Eleanor Ward lives below her "shop," the Stable Gallery, and her residence is reached by circular staircase. A painted plywood wall houses books and objects. Panels of light on the top and bottom shelves illuminate the pre-Columbian art, antiquities and modern boxes by Joseph Cornell. John W. Bedenkapp designed the room and Indy, a Welsh corgi, relishes the right to sit on the Spanish Victorian chair or French provincial sofa.

The entertainment center dominating the passageway between living and dining rooms in Joseph and Muriel Buttinger's home, disappears behind white and yellow laminated plastic sliding doors when not in use. When open, elaborate hi-fi and a bar is ready for use. The sound section in the foreground has, at top, loudspeakers behind an inclined pandamus-covered panel. Amplifiers, tuner and lighting are directly below. The waist-high counter lifts up providing access to the record player and tape recorder. Record storage is to the left and, like the most of interior of the wall unit, is of walnut. The bar at far left, has a plastic counter, storage for bottles and glasses. Designed by Felix Augenfeld.

Off the concert stage, Isaac Stern's music life begins here. The violinist practices here (as do his two children) and holds impromptu concerts seated on the violin-shaped chair that was designed by Fornasetti, an Italian artist. Storage for music, violins, bows is provided for in shelves behind the closed oak doors, left, and behind sliding doors across the tops of the cabinets. Hi-fi components, including a professional tape recorder and eight speakers, and record storage are at center. Books on music are arranged on open walnut shelves, right. Designed by Oskar Barshak.

Drama in design depends on the sum of all the parts. Herbert Beckhard, architect, proves this in striking fashion with a 17-foot storage wall, which is the focal point of his living room. In the center of the wall is a photomural that Mr. Beckhard constructed using photographs that he took while traveling with his wife and family. The cabinets directly below house hi-fi components and a bar with such details as the knobs of the amplifier and tuner left exposed, turning them into decorative assets. The record changer is reached by lifting up a panel above the speaker. The exposed shelves hold books and art objects, and the enclosed cabinets, such as those at the top of the unit, provide storage space for cameras, film and photographs. Interior sections and bar doors are of oil-finished walnut. All the other wood was sprayed with a hard white lacquer. Color is furnished by the books, the bright blue wall leading to the children's wing and the warm wood tones of the cypress ceiling. The floor is bluestone. Marcel Breuer chairs and Knoll sofas complete the picture.

The Living Wall

Casual though it may seem, the jagged arrangement of
the bookshelves here and the exposed speakers was deftly
planned by Ludovico Magistretti for the Italian villa of Franco
Cassina, one of Europe's largest furniture producers. The
painted shelves supported by enameled metal brackets are visually balanced by the bull's eye faces of the stereophonic speakers. Mr. Magistretti, an architect, chose to use the mantel of
the white-washed brick fireplace as a shelf for the tape recorder,
amplifiers and turntable. The furnishings were also designed
by Mr. Magistretti and made by Mr. Cassina. A devotee of the
works of Le Corbusier—Mr. Cassina manufactures reproduc-
tions of the late architect's furniture—the owner also hung a
drawing by the architect over the fireplace.

Light and Lightness

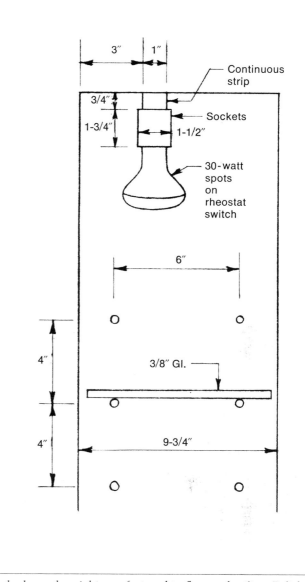

¾-inch plywood uprights are fastened to floor and ceiling. Polished plate glass shelves are ⅜ inches thick and are adjustable. Holes for shelves drilled in uprights are 4 inches apart. Shelf supports are brushed chrome plugs. 30-watt par spots fit in round sockets, are controlled by dimmer.

On the adjustable plate glass shelves here and in two other rooms of their Manhattan apartment are books related to the many interests of Mr. and Mrs. Clyde R. Rich Jr. Among the couple's acquisitions are American Indian dolls, Egyptian sculptures dating to 3,000 B.C., a 50-million-year-old fish fossil found in Wyoming, Shaker boxes, old fans, ancient Greek and Roman stones and Japanese scrolls. Mr. Rich, an architectural consultant to the Museum of Modern Art, illuminates this collection and books on art, history and archeology with 30-watt spotlights strung across the top of the niche. The recess was made by duplicating the left column with a second, fake, plywood column at right, thereby giving the room symmetry.

Country

The simplest solutions are often the best—a wall-to-wall installation of bookshelves under the windows, a floor-to-ceiling bookcase for records and books. Nothing could be simpler, nothing more effective for this living room in the home of Mr. and Mrs. Calvin Tomkins. The staff writer of The New Yorker and his wife inherited the shelving from previous tenants of this century-old farmhouse in Sneden's Landing, Palisades, N.Y., and didn't wish to change a thing. Speakers stand exposed on a shelf and under the window. The turntable sits uncovered in the bookcase at right. In a room where the plank floors, Delaware Valley ladder back chairs, sawbuck table and 17th century desk are as forthright as the sun washing the oriental carpet, the modern amenities are as they should be.

City

For Mr. and Mrs. Edward Tishman's home, Philip Enfield designed a plaster wall with niches for books and built-in cabinets for the hi-fi system and television set. The illuminated niches are 11 inches high and 10 inches deep. A walnut platform extends the length of the wall, supporting the sofa and hi-fi cabinet. Hi-fi components, seen through the glass panels of the cabinet, are reached by raising the lid on which Mr. Tishman, a realtor, sits to adjust the television set. From this position he can pull the set forward and swivel it for TV-viewing anywhere in the room.

Furniture and Wall Systems

A mobile book tower which shrinks or grows as the owner wishes is Joe Cesare Colombo's conception of a library on wheels. The Milanese designer constructed his oiled walnut bookcase in the round. Layers can be arranged as the owner wills to accommodate books, magazines, phonograph records and hi-fi equipment between the dividers. When it comes time to move, the baseball-sized casters carry the load.

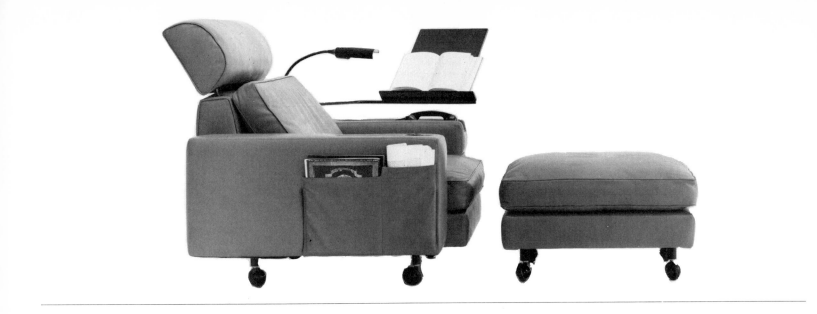

Comfort

A chair so comfortable that it holds the sitter through a single reading of War and Peace must also provide more than basic needs. Amenities added by Cini Boeri, a Milanese architect-designer to his leather-covered easy chair are a reading stand and light, pocket for tucking magazines and newspapers, a hidden storage compartment under a chair arm for snacks or chocolates and a built-in note pad, ashtray and, for those who want distraction, a telephone.

Convertible

A pair of Fiat doors on this bookcase-buffet open on shelves, close as easily as those on the car. The fantasy creation was conceived and executed by Ugo Sterpini, a Rome painter, and Fabio De Sanctis, a Rome architect. Instead of wheels, this auto-like storage unit stands pat on lions' feet.

Cubes

Plywood table boxes small enough to carry about, function as portable bookcases, end tables, or to hold bar or hi-fi equipment. Designed by John Way Jr., an architect, the cubes have oak plywood adjustable shelves edged in oak veneer. The outside frames are enameled white. Casters at the base make them movable.

Return of the Glass Doors

The revival of the glass-doored bookcase is a far cry from those found in homes 30 years ago. In these wood-framed glass towers by Tobia and Afra Scarpa for Stildomus of Italy, the glass dissuades dust but invites looking. The cases are held together by special angle plates in the frames.

Mobile

A low, rosewood coffee table is fitted under the top surface with book, record, bar and other storage. The 32-inch square table measures 18 inches high, rolls about on golf-ball-size casters. Vertical dividers are adjustable in shelves on this Scandinavian import.

Snack Time

Ash table delivers double dividends. With the book rest down the table serves as a cocktail table. With it up it becomes a living room lectern and still offers space for a cup of coffee and a piece of apple pie. The table was designed by Edward J. Wormley for Dunbar.

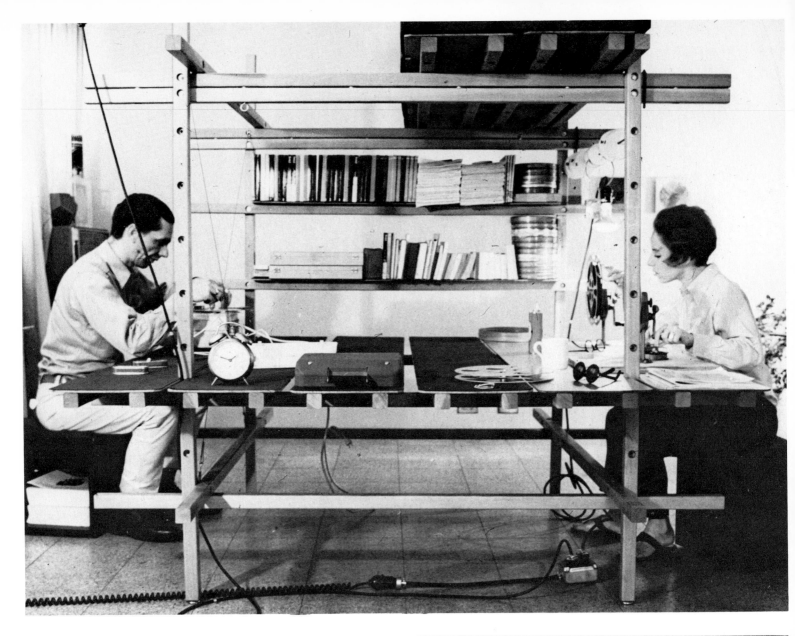

Well, It's Home

An unassuming pile of lumber rises to become Kenneth Isaacs' Living Structure, an environment for working, dining, sleeping and, of course, reading. A skeleton structure of 2-by-2's come with Masonite pallets for the bookshelves, sleeping and work surfaces. The jungle gym-like room within a room disassembles by removing the bolts and deflating the air mattresses. Mr. Isaacs considers the design as one solution in a mobile society where the space squeeze is felt in homes everywhere.

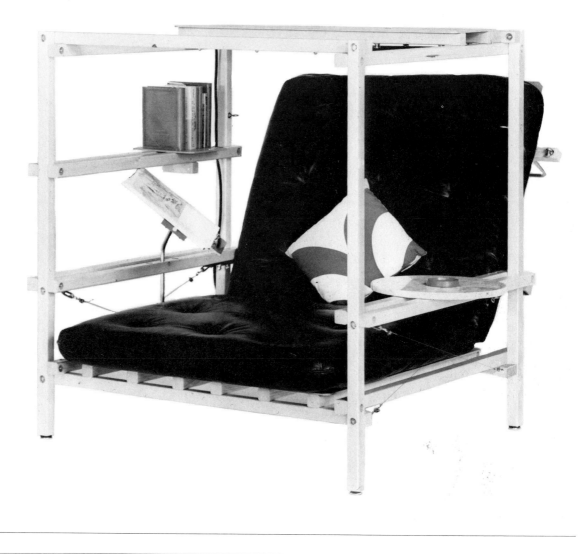

Cubicle environment for reading is a miniature version of Kenneth Isaacs room-sized multi-purpose structure. The wood-slatted cube comes equipped with a bookshelf, reading stand and light. Comfortable cushions pad seat and back, which adjusts to the sitter's desire.

Books appear to float on air but are in fact resting on wood shelves, secured in place by notched acrylic plastic sides. The Swedish String Design system is installed quite simply by affixing metal hardware to the walls, attaching the plastic sides to the hardware and hooking wood shelves into the notched sides. The eminently flexible system can be adjusted so that shelves are placed at desired heights. Imported by Fabry Associates, Inc.

Threaded rods used as poles between plywood shelves were used by Lord Snowden for a book and hi-fi installation in London. Here Michael Boys, the photographer, adapts the idea using stainless steel, 3-foot-long rods measuring 1-inch in diameter. The shelves are held in place with 1¼-inch steel washers and 1-inch brass nuts. The holes in the shelving were drilled by brace and bit.

Everything hinges on the knuckle in today's ingenious new shelving systems. In this Raum Technik System, the knuckle is plastic, the shape is as shown or 12 other forms to hold the two, three or four panels together. Panels for this German-made shelving and art display equipment are of hardboard or clear or smoked glass. Although no single installation could prove it, its designers Hans Staeger and Manfred Malzacher of Stuttgart claim there are 4,095 ways to combine the parts. The system is imported by Beylerian, Ltd.

Coupled

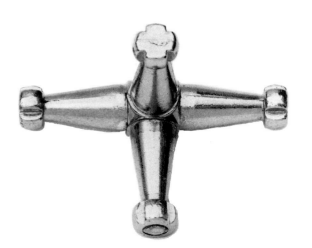

Metal knuckles lock the Abstracta tubing system together to support on glass or hardboard shelves the contents of a library or art collection. Designed by Poul Cadovius of Denmark, the system comes in either black or chromed metal tubing of different lengths. Only a smooth knob is visible at the corners of the free standing units when they are assembled.

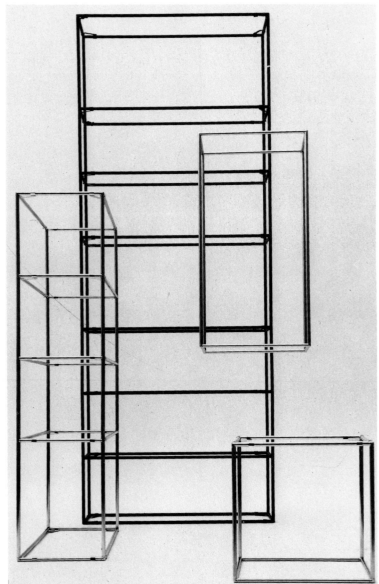

Stacked

Lacquered wood cubicles are locked in place by anodized aluminum joints in this Tecno of Milan system. In this case the joint is a rod joining a triangular or square metal disc. The cubicles have angled corners to accept the joints and come in two sizes—14½ inches square or 14½ by 29½ inches. All units are 10½ inches deep. Called Prisma, the system was designed by Eduardo Vittoria, an Italian architect.

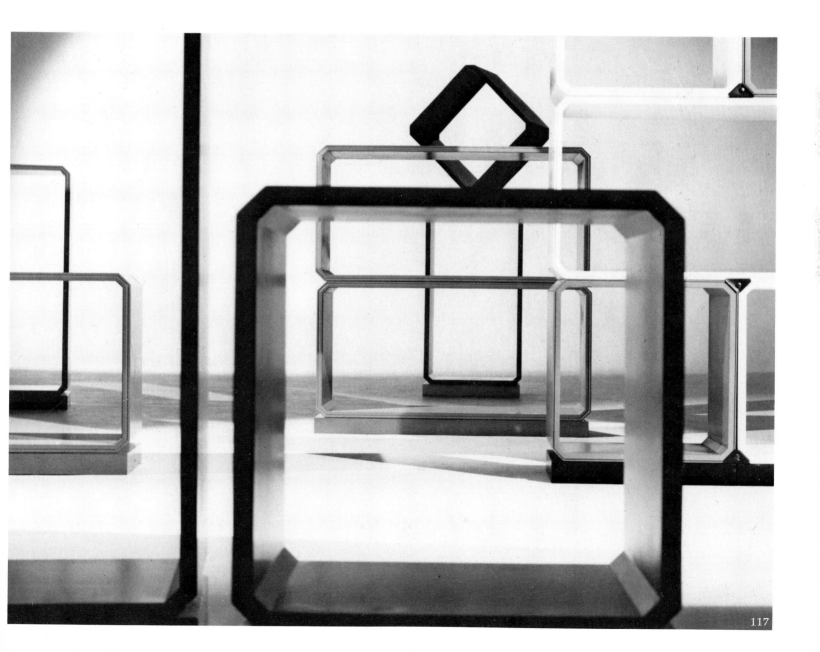

Man-made Tree

Wendell Castle's weighty walnut library sculpture grows like a tree with bookshelf and twin seats branching out of the base. The Rochester-based sculptor-turned-craftsman hews his designs from solid woods, laminating each one-inch-thick sheet together layer by layer with a jeweler's precision. Lighting is also incorporated in the library design which is 7½ feet tall, 6½ feet wide.

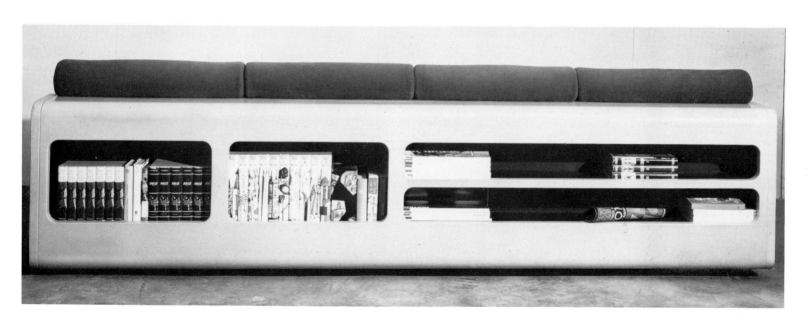

In the Rear

The perfect end to a sofa where many people curl up with a book, is to have the bookshelf incorporated in the design. Cesare M. Casati of Milan did just that in this four-seater design. The sofa also comes equipped with a radio, ash trays and cigarette lighter.

Where to Find It

The following is a list of architects, designers, manufacturers or
retail sales sources where further information regarding the installations
shown can be obtained:

76. Ulrich Franzen, 555 Madison Avenue, New York, N.Y.

76. John W. Bedenkapp, 425 East 51st Street, New York, N.Y.

79. Zographos Designs Ltd., 510 Madison Avenue, New York, N.Y.

79. John W. Bedenkapp, 425 East 51st Street, New York, N.Y.

80. Clyde R. Rich Jr., 156 East 52d Street, New York, N.Y.

81. Lanier Graham, M. H. De Young Museum, Golden Gate Park, San Francisco, Calif.

82. Kason Hardware Corporation, Binghamton, N.Y. 13902

83. Royal System, Inc., 1130 Third Avenue, New York, N.Y.

84, 85. Laurie & Stanley Maurer, 172 Amity Street, Brooklyn, N.Y.

86, 87. Adolf Knüppel, Wilhelmstrasse 61, 44 Munster, Westphalia, West Germany

87. Yung Wang, 155 West 91st Street, New York, N.Y.

89. Frederick R. Gorree, 109 East 19th Street, New York, N.Y.

92. Don Eliasen, Duffy, Inc., 53 Park Place, New York, N.Y.

93. Ulrich Franzen, 555 Madison Avenue, New York, N.Y.

96. John W. Bedenkapp, 425 East 51st Street, New York, N.Y.

98. John W. Bedenkapp, 425 East 51st Street, New York, N.Y.

99. Felix Augenfeld, 201 East 66th Street, New York, N.Y.

100. Herbert Beckhard, Marcel Breuer & Associates, 635 Madison Avenue, New York, N.Y.

102, 103. Clyde R. Rich Jr., 156 East 52d Street, New York, N.Y.

105. Philip Enfield Designs, 353 East 78th Street, New York, N.Y.

107. Mrs. Joe Cesare Colombo, via F. Argelati, 36/B Milan, Italy

108, 109. Fabio De Sanctis and Ugo Sterpini, via A. Stoppani 10, Rome, Italy

110. Stildomus, via Laurentina Km. 27, Pomezia Rome, Italy

110. Modern Furniture Department, Macy's, Herald Square, New York, N.Y.

111. Dunbar Furniture Corp., 305 East 63d Street, New York, N.Y.

111, 112. Kenneth Isaacs, 333 East 43d Street, New York, N.Y.

115. Beylerian Ltd., 253 Fifth Avenue, New York, N.Y.

116. Abstracta System, 101 Park Avenue, New York, N.Y., available at Bonniers, 605 Madison Avenue, New York, N.Y.

117. Tecno, via Bigli 22, Milan, Italy

118. Wendell Castle, 18 Maple Street, Scottsville, N.Y.

119. Cesare M. Casati, Editoriale Domus, via Monte di Pietà 15, Milan, Italy

Book Design: Louis Silverstein

Cover Design: John Condon

Production: Planned Production

Photo Credits

Photographed by Duane Michals unless otherwise noted below:

Morley Baer, page 51
Aldo Ballo, pages 107, 108 top
Michael Boys, page 114
Casali-Domus, page 110
Casali, page 119
Julian Cohen, page 61
Dainesi/Pinto, page 64
Robert Damora, page 76
Carla de Benedetti, page 101
Alexander Georges, pages 70 right, 71, 91, 99 top
William Kennedy, pages 27 left, 50
Jan Klein, page 114
Edmund Y. Lee, page 42
Herbert C. McDonald, page 67
Norman McGrath, pages 11, 12, 29, 33, 47, 57 top, 109
Hans Namuth, pages 96, 100, 113
The New York Times
    Bill Aller, pages 18, 25, 31, 35, 87, 115, 116
    Don Charles, page 104
    Gene Maggio, pages 22 left, 34 below left and right,
    58, 59, 81 top, 97, 98 left
Jowa Parisini, pages 27 right, 38-39
Louis Reens, page 92
Robert Riggs, page 13 bottom
Ezra Stoller, page 65
Sulick Studio, page 110
Mike Willett, page 114
Williams/Pinto, pages 13 top, 40, 57 bottom
Zweitasch, page 86

About the Author

Privileged peering into other people's houses has occupied Rita Reif for almost two decades as a reporter for *The New York Times.* One of her specialties is reporting what people do with their homes to make them more attractive and more comfortable and convenient.

In this capacity, Mrs. Reif has observed and reported the growth of home libraries and the burgeoning appetite for art and hi-fi installations. Her interest has been both professional and personal.

At home in Manhattan she has charge over five libraries—the music wall where her composer husband Paul keeps his scores and recordings, the book walls of her two sons (see page 25), the family library in the living room and the shelves in her own home office.

She confesses that try as she will she still cannot part with the books that saw her through her undergraduate years at Fordham University and her master's degree at Columbia University. Then there are all the volumes consulted in the writing of her two other books, *The Antique Collector's Guide To Styles and Prices* and *Treasure Rooms of America's Mansions, Manors and Houses.* As in other homes, it is a fact of life that the books keep piling up.